# INSURRECTION

First Edition    First Printing
Insurrection
Copyright © 2006 by Julius Kane

Address inquiries to:

Maverick-Publishing Co.
8206 Hampton Blvd, suite 281
Norfolk, Virginia 23505
(757) 227-7274


ISBN:  0-9785056-0-3



Cover designed by LaRhonda Quinn

Typesetting by LaRhonda Quinn

THIS BOOK IS DEDICATED TO PEOPLE
EVERYWHERE… DEDICATED TO ANYONE
WHO'S WITHOUT A VOICE BUT NEEDS TO BE
HEARD…. DEDICATED TO TWO GREAT
TEACHERS, MRS CHARMAINE TURNER AND
MR. RON WHITENACK.
THANK YOU SO MUCH!

# Contents

Scream

Fantastic lies create a sensational stir-
while grains of truth fall on deaf ears.

Is anybody listening?

I FEEL THE NEED TO **S-C-R-E-A-M!**
"LISTEN TO ME. I'VE GOT SOMETHING
IMPORTANT TO SAY!"

Allow me to step onto your stage.
I need to hear my voice and know that you're
listening.
I need to feel sunlight on my face too!

An airplane hears its' echo across the sky.
A tractor hears its' roar upon the open field.
Even a dog can hear its' bark crack the midnight air.

Like the moon demanding the clouds-
"Get out of my way!"

I need to be seen.
I need to enlighten every dark, unmentioned corner
of this America.

Aint that what voices are for?
To shout …. To scream …. To be heard?

....Now, I don't want your scripted dialog clogging up people ears. I'll bite your hand if you try to put words in my mouth.

I swear I got to **S-C-R-E-A-M!**

"Here I am! ……Notice me!"
I'm a member of this world.

I'm born …. I suffer …. I'll die!
I've got issues that need to be heard, need to be felt,
Need to be lifted off of my shoulders.

Now I got to **S-C-R-E-A-M!**
"HERE I AM!"

Is anybody listening?

## AIDS Is Worth More Alive, Than Dead!

AIDS is worth more alive, than dead!
Medicine in America arrives with a hefty price tag.

Corporate drug dealers price gouge our sick
while our government turns its' head,
Mama told me it's because they both sleep in the
same bed.

No matter how much the people of this world plead,
nothing supersedes Anglo-Saxon greed.

The new American pharmaceutical slogan should
read:
"If you can't afford our medicine, then don't get the
damn disease."

# Mothers' **Of War**

Big wars in little countries see...

Mothers' of war
Identify
And
Collect
Their dead sons
From the battlefield.
And-
They did the same
For their son's
Fathers before them.

Young women
With Children
Who will grow up Without
Their fathers, Cry and
Remember-As they dig
Their fingers Through
Scorching sand for
Keepsakes, And ask why?

Casualties and losses
Are accepted in battle-
But
Unacceptable
At the negotiating table.
In a room filled with
So called
Dignitiaries.

And when the war
Is over
And enough blood has
Been spilled,
Money and property
Are the only things that change
Hands.

Presidents, Ambassadors, and
Generals are the only people
Who smile and take pictures
Because
Careers and reputations
Are built off wars.

And all the women who lost
Their husbands and sons
For someone else's
Idealism-
Don't have any say-so
About what happens the next
Day in their little country.

The only decision they are
Allowed to make is where they
Want their husbands and sons
To be buried.

# Travel Abroad Under An Assumed Country!

Think I'll take me a trip around the world,
I need to get away and stretch my legs a bit.

Stop in Cuba
Wave goodbye to a couple of exiles.
America offers them amnesty.
They say no,
And burn our flag.

Awful hot here in Columbia.
Think I'll take a swim.
Fo' I can get my toes in the water good,
Some boy on the beach with an assault rifle
Is cussin'
And burnin' our flag.

Pull up to a four star restaurant in France.
Um, um, um
Smell that cuisine!
Get up and peep in the kitchen.
Now I got to leave.
I can't eat here!
Two of the chefs are cookin' a stew-
And burnin' our flag.

You know I had to take me a boat trip
On that fine Queen Mary 2.
Let me get off in Spain.
Buy me some souvenirs and look around.
The shop keepers see me comin' a block away.
They lock their doors

And burn our flag.

Guess I'll caravan across the Holy Land.
What a trip!
That's a lot of walkin'
Got to rest my tired feet.
Can't sit here too long though.
The man leading the caravan is giving a speech,
And burnin' our flag.

Landed in Pakistan.
Think I'll take a camel ride.
Never done that before.
Never even been on a horse.
Lawd! Help me get off this thing!
The man on the camel next to me is naked,
And burnin' our flag.

Well, ready to get back home now.
But I'm delayed at the airport in Rome.
The plane can't take off.
There's a bunch of folks on the runway.
Guess what they doin'?
That's right!
Burnin' our flag.

# Carnivorous

What animal am I?
Who will never cry
Yet make others shed bitter tears
I hate
I loathe
And thumb my nose
At enemies and thrive on their fears
I walk on two legs
And have two eyes
But can only look straight ahead.

What am I?

With a serpents tongue I talk
And as slippery as an eel I walk
Through the darkness of streets paved in blood
My cold heart is numb
My tortured soul overcome
By the sheer hatred I have inside for you.

Again I ask, what am I?

What beast am I
Who lies in wait
To devour your wives and children

With savage accuracy I'll plan your fate
Then for months I sleep and hibernate.
Unlike men
I dwell in darkness and shadows
Like a nomad
I migrate place to place
Stalking unsuspecting prey.
I don't hesitate to kill
Then disappear at will
They haven't caged me yet
I am an animal no zoo can keep for a pet
If by now you haven't guessed
They call me evil-
Animalist-
Terrorist.

# Church and State

The Buddhist may say –
"Your religion doesn't work for me, I need to see my God!"

The Atheist says to the Buddhist –
"Your God is carved from wood and is only fit for a fire."

The Christian says to the Atheist-
"Even you are made in God's image."

But I saw that same Christian scowl at the sight of a Muslim.

The Muslim bows before Allah and vows to kill all infidels,

which includes all Jehovah Witnesses and Catholics.

The Catholic priests are supposed to exonerate all killers from

sin. And if he has enough money will guarantee him a place in

Heaven next to Jesus, who's probably standing next to a Jew.

The Jewish man says-
"God never had a son so there was no Jesus who was
sacrificed by Jews."

So he must shun the origin of Christianity and ask-
"Does God love the Baptist, Methodist, or Protestant more
than me?"

Religious battle lines were formed long ago and each
denomination claims to be on the winning side. Across this
country and around this world church and state have publicly

been holding hands. God Inc. has joined the fortune 500, yet managed to retain its non-profit status. Men who claim to be friends with God seek to rule and force their ideals upon millions. But if they're going to force us to listen to such rhetoric, why don't we all just make God President!

# The Kindest Victim

The Kindest Victim Never Says A Word!

Inner scars are hard to see. You and I know
a quiet victim says-
"You're excused for hurting me"

The kindest victim may not scream,
but can at least whisper a name.
You're not brave for keeping it in
while your offender offends
again and again.

See, no two victims die the same.
But most victims don't die from being victimized,
most victims die of shame.

# Insult To Injury

Assault and berating
can leave a woman
with a torn dress.
Violence and rage
can leave her head
a bloody mess.

Force and aggression
can leave her insides bruised
while self-blame and pride
yield very little clues.

When life or death
forms inside her womb,
taking away her right to choose
only pours salt on a festering wound.

# One in **every two** family's

Insanity parades its face
around my house
and I can't get any rest.

Psychiatrists
all offer one solution-
Fill them up with Prozac.

We all know that problem's
back again.
Mirrors shatter, dishes being flung,
someone needs to take their medicine.

Profanity and slurs break the silence
of a perfect afternoon.
spots stain the wall from food
being thrown across the room.

Arguments and fights erupt
while the children stand in the doorway and cry.
Onlookers stop and stare
through the screen door
as they hurry on by.

Loyalty is the posture of insanity.
Thank God my wife stayed next to me.
After all the places I've been
I think her love worked better
than any of their medicine.

# A letter from the Writer

Dear Reader,

When you forget what happened yesterday,
the same thing can happen tomorrow.
Maybe not to you,
but to someone else, somewhere else.
People who don't want you to bring up your history
are embarrassed by the role they played in it.
Others just don't give a damn about your past struggle
or the ripple effect it's had on your life,
and could possibly have on your future.
You not only have a right to remember,
but you have an obligation to remember.
Never forget your family, your heritage, your ancestors,
who lived, bled, and died
so that you may freely and without fear
read these verses.

Sincerely

Julius Kane

PS. I ain't gonna let you forget!

# Injustice

The American penal system is a beast. The American justice system is its master – Determined to keep Minorities on her leash.

# Demographically Challenged

Demographically challenged,
always on someone's list.
burdened down,
by all this damn analysis.

Demonized,
in order to symbolize
the negative ingredient in this melting pot.
Extensively scrutinized,
as the major player in a government plot.

Been economically betrayed.
so I'm negatively portrayed
as the villian
no matter what scenario is given.

Categorized,
by my responses and reactions to your actions.
all aspects of my life have been media intensified.
work ethic scrutinized.
family life, demoralized.
you won't believe how many times I've been denied.

Economy/paternity/education/incarceration
you pick the list
I guarantee,
my name is all over it.

Still-
Constantly hated.
You lone, demographic statistic.

# You've Taken My Hip-Hop And Gone

You've taken my hip-hop and gone
First
You tried to ban it
Because you couldn't understand it.
Found out-
Your kids can't live without it.
I'm a minority but my
Culture is the majority Of
Everything you see
And everything your children want to be a part of.
Now you want to embrace me
To claim all my royalties.
You Master of Economic Slavery.
You got me peepin' in the windows
Of buildings that I built.
You keep me out of meetings and offices
That I filled, with my sweat.
You Corporate Pimp! You corrupt
everything  you touch – pretending like you
L-O-V-E me so much.

You also took my R&B
You mimic my dance moves,
Develop white groups to try and sound like me.
But they ain't me!
Made me sell my soul to sell my soul music.
Made a name off my back-
Then turned around and put me out back.
You done gone and put your stamp on everything
that's black.

But one day I'm gone take my culture back
I'm gone find a black lawyer
Who can explain the fine print,
Gone let me know where all my money went.
I'm gone get educated so you can't exploit me
again. And once this information sinks in, we
gone make Langston proud of us again,
just wait'til you see me again.

# Symbols

Nappy hair
thick lips
always
dry, seldom licked.
Broad shoulders
Wide-
Curious eyes
Deep
Dark skin
Considered unwise
Big barefeet
Corns and bunions
Strong and fertile
Make babies
By the dozens
Chicken/ collards/ chitterlings/ cotton
Broken down house in Alabama
Abandoned,
But not forgotten.
Jazz/ guitar/ trumpet/ blues
Dancin raisins
In papas old
And worn out shoes.
Mammie/ yes sir / fetchen/ fixin
Dragged into a new century
Where we still fight and bleed
Ugly innuendoes wrapped around my neck
Make it hard for me to breathe.
Don't take my word for it
Look around
And I'm sure you'll agree-
Over a hundred years of waiting
And those poor symbols
Ain't never been freed.

## These Dark Hands

These dark hands have touched
And touched
And touched
So much.

In kitchens
On pots and pans they've rubbed
And rubbed
And rubbed
So much.

These slave hands know cotton
And grain
And tobacco
And thorns
And dirt
And mud.
With knuckles bald and bloody
They've wiped a river of sweaty tears from my face.

These dark hands have clapped and clapped
To old Negro spirituals
Held candles at tearful vigils
Practiced and taught old African rituals.

These tired hands wear scars

And scrapes
And burns
And welts
From whips
And straps and belts.

These dry fingers know the feel of the cold steel cage
Of jail bars
Branding scars
Segregated box cars.
Traveling through the south in the thick of night
In desperate flight
They've taken me from that plantation.
Through forests
And fields
And rivers
And lakes.
Through dirt
And grime
And rocks.
They take-
Refuge
In cabins
And cellars
And barns
And crates.

These dark hands know trouble and fear
And pain
And hate
Which is why they tremble and shake
And make these fingers turn into fists
That broke the cuffs from around these wrists.

These strong hands have grabbed and clawed
And smacked
And smashed the skull of a vicious bloodhound.
While others gave up, my smell was never found.
In the scent of it's guts and urine I washed and
Washed
And waited
Alone
And cried
And cried
Until the slave hunters were gone.

These blind hands have done my bidding
Willingly
Literally
They have squeezed the last breath from the neck
Of my masters flesh.
His bones moaned beneath their palms.

Stronger and stronger

No longer a beast in his stable
I eat
And I eat
And I feast
At the head of my own table

These dark hands
And fingers
And arms
And legs
And head
Can clap
And sing
And laugh
And hope
And dream
Of so many things

And this is why I love these dark hands
That have touched
And touched
And touched
So much.

# Say, Brother

"The most effective way to exploit black people is to make them exploit each other."

# 2 Divided By 1

His skin is not as dark as mine
so he says
"your fate is not my own."

His mama and daddy
Look like my mama and daddy
Still he says
"your fate is not my own."

Because I sleep in the slave quarters
and he sleeps in the master's house
he says
"your fate is not my own."

When master's liquor turned up missing
they tied us both to the same tree.
Split his back wide open
just like me.

And when we finished bleeding
we both put our clothes back on.
I went back to the slave quarters
and he went back to the masters house
and he again said,
"See, your fate is not my own!"

# Black Muse Inspires Works Of Blackness

Black muse inspires bronze statues and portraits of
urban sunsets in renewal. Make writers create verses
that sing of proud black mamas and

of strong black daddies. Black muse inside the voice
of the actor, inspires the playwright, who inspires
the producer, who aspires to make such a

grand and joyful noise. Black muse breathes life
into a poet's ordinary words, causing them to stretch,
run and jump off their pages and into

boundless possibilities. Black muse assumes the form
of my little girl – inspiring me to transcend my dead
end job, in hopes she may someday be inspired

to dream, achieve and succeed. Thank God for little
things. Thank God for black muses.

# Remembering Elsa

In 1855, Elsa was notoriously pregnant and there was no man to step forward and relieve her shame. People would sometimes whisper and point when they saw Elsa on the street. Usually she walked alone, seemingly oblivious, quietly gazing up at the sky,-like expecting rain to fall, or staring down at the ground – as if to be deep in thought. Elsa would have been

the apple of any father's eye. She was tall, thin, and very beautiful. Her smooth bronze skin had been ever so gently kissed by the sun. Her eyes sparkled and spoke to you without her uttering a single word. Her long, thick, flowing hair was mostly kept in ribbons or ties but often covered her high cheekbones. If you ever heard Elsa's voice, it was said to be nothing short of angelic. And her walk, her walk was elegant. Not a sway, or switch, or swagger. She simply had an unrehearsed polish

in her stride. Elsa had no family of which to speak. She never knew her mother or father, and could barely remember the faces of her brothers and sisters. She lost them when she was only five. Her only kinship was to those who shared the same skin as she, the same workload, the same monotony. Hers was indeed a lonely

state of being. Folks said Elsa was Mr. Thompson's favorite. So for a time, he treated her better than all the other workers, which fueled a lot of resentment. At a time of great indifference, everyone looked at her differently.

No one wanted to befriend Mr. Thompson's favorite.
Some – because of envy.
Others – because of fear. Mr. Thompson was known to be
intemperate and watchful over his favorites. Elsa slept in
the main house whenever Mr. Thompson's wife was
away. Often Mr. Thompson gave her extra food, warm
clothes, shoes, socks, blankets, and fruit baskets. Gifts she
dare not refuse. He even sent her into town for supplies
riding horseback, while the other workers were

on foot next to her. In mid winter, when her
stomach started to show, there was a huge shift in Mr.
Thompson's demeanor. Elsa wasn't ordered to the main
house anymore. The work she use to do was given to
another girl. New meat for Mr. Thompson's old bones. In
fact, extra food and hand-me-downs immediately stopped
coming. Elsa was relieved. She never wished for nor
wanted Mr. Thompson's attention. Now she worked on
his farm – and in his fields, and sometimes in the kitchen
of the main house. Her face was stoic and her mood as
sullen as always. She rarely said a word. Hardly spoke to
anyone. She maintained her own little world of seclusion.
Not so much as a curse parted her lips. She never smiled
– always serious. The load on her back was heavy, but
like a little mule, a so;emt Elsa never asked anyone for
help. Sun up to sun down, dizzy, or out of breath – she
always

carried her own weight. Elsa received no pre-natal
care. No doctor came by to visit. No hospital examination
ever took place. Such convenience didn't exist in her
world. There was only a nod, or glance, followed by short

exchanges of advice from the older women who worked next to her everyday. One late night in her modest abode

not much bigger than a shed, far removed from the lights, music, clamor, and southern charm of the main house – Elsa felt her water break. Alone in the darkness, with only the glow from a flickering candle - without so much as a midwife to hold her hand – Elsa cried, and screamed, and pushed, and gave life to a healthy baby boy. And in that instant, love touched her heart. Elsa never cared about her hardships or seclusion, or how the other workers treated her – or how Mr. Thompson touched her, because it was all she ever knew. But for the first time in her young life something actually mattered. And it was there in the depth of her blackness, in the thick void of a room with no walls and no warmth – and certainly no happiness – Elsa actually … smiled!

--Elsa lay still in the puddle of blood that soaked her pallet. There was nothing more she could do. She felt a kind of relief, like a burden was soon to be lifted from her shoulders. She was resigned to her fate. She held her baby close to her breast and poured a lifetime of her love into a few precious hours. Elsa laid motionless all night in darkness and pain – quietly watching the candle –like her life – burn out. The next morning when Elsa didn't come out to work, a few of the women went to rouse her. They found Elsa with her face close to her crying baby. He kicked and screamed-and his voice was strong and resounding. But there was no life at all left in Elsa's young fifteen-year-old body. Her hands were clinched tightly around her newborn. They looked like the hands of a sixty-year old woman, more so than those of a young girl. They were bruised, cut, ashy, wrinkled and smelled of dry blood. The women removed the crying baby from Elsa's lifeless arms. They cleaned him, clothed him, even named him – and gave him to a local woman of whom it was believed to be barren and who seemed to adore him instantly.

Some of the field hands put Elsa's body in an unmarked grave. They took turns digging as they so often had done. The older women dressed Elsa up real nice before they placed her inside that box. But there was no funeral. Mr. Thompson didn't allow his workers to have funerals. He said it slowed down production. So there would be no sad songs. No preacher to speak any kind words. And certainly no flowers were sent down from the main house. None of the men and women who worked next to Elsa could read or write so there was no way to mark her remains. And really, if they could so much as write her name, there would probably be no family who would ever come to grieve.

In all the years they knew her, no one had ever seen Elsa smile, or laugh, or swear, or burst into tears. She remained an enigma to them all. And so Elsa's life story passed into obscurity. Many years went by. The story of Elsa's life and pain changed from time to time – person to person. Details became blurred until there's hardly any facts left about the short life and lonely death of a little slave girl named Elsa. A bright light that never shined. But isn't hers a life worth mentioning? And if I were to say a few words for Elsa, They would be:

Goodbye beautiful black child. I know that in heaven your smile is so bright the angels can't stare directly at you.

Goodbye beautiful black child. I know that your new family really loves you.

Bless you child, for being so strong.

Bless you child, for being ours.

Bless you, great, great grandma Elsa –

Bless you!

# History Repeats Itself

From a podium, deep in the heart of this
American south, a familiar voice breaks
the silence.
Dressed in red, white, and blue
his raspy tone cracks the ears
of every man, woman, and child of color.

This stranger's stirring rhetoric is bash,
cynical, and forceful.
He's making his conservative and liberal
views known, as inquisitive crowds
of listeners begin to swarm.

Suddenly, an old woman recognizes him.
Fingers point,
tongues whisper,
and faces become enraged.
He has been identified
as the long forgotten, wicked stepfather
of every black man, woman, and child
spawned of this American South.

Every cornbread eating, discontent negro
who walked out of a cotton field
knows his name.
Jim Crow is who he be.
And he's back to lay claim to what's his.

His propaganda is patriotism through
fear, false representation and mis-education.
He also specializes in the misappropriation of funds.
He put his brand of religion
into politics
and fused his politics

with religion.

He knows how to say what people want to hear.

"Where have you been all these years Mr. Jim Crow?"
a reporter yells through the crowd.

"Well boys, I ain't blocking the entrance to schools anymore.
I want them to go to school. What good is school without
qualified teachers?"

"But where have you been?"

"I've been behind the scenes. I'm nationwide now! I'm still a
little pissed off about that whole back of the bus thing, but I
made up for it. If they're all in prison how the hell can they sit
in front of a bus? Just who do you think invented those
mandatory sentencing guidelines?"

Jim Crow.
That champion of inequality – super lobbyist.

"I helped make cross burning legal in Virginia….Did away
with affirmative action and made police brutality an
institution out there in California….Made a mockery of the
public school system in New York….Stole me a presidential
election in Florida….And that was me behind the scenes in
New Orleans….Think about it….Please…. Who else would
have named a bunch of black hurricane victims –
Refugees?"

As defiant as ever, he's back at Center Stage.

Standing tall at the podium,
Jim Crow wants your vote.

"How will you win in 2008?"
another reporter asked.

"Yeah, times have changed a little. The all-purpose negro has disappeared. The new negro has emerged. But he still wears the old scars and bruises I gave him. But his children have never met me, can't you tell…Done changed their names to African Americans. Huh! They don't have a clue about who I am. Plus, I'm better organized now. No more will you see the tobacco chewing / fat / pig / redneck in front of the camera. We have the new / young / hip / educated / Wall Street / computer savvy / businessman on your television screen. And he's both Republican and Democrat."

"But can he win their votes?"
the reporter follows up.

"He knows what time it is! He's got me standing back stage. I taught him how to speak the urban language. I gave him an interpreter to untangle all that hip – hop terminology. I've equipped him with enough money and connections to unravel all that empowerment bullshit. Oh yeah, I'm going to win. And I'll do it by any means necessary!"

--Jim Crow ….. Coming to a city near you!

# Company Policy

Young black boy
doesn't try to win
because he knows
the game is rigged.

Still,
he participates blindly
hoping for a level playing field.

He tries his hardest
to stay in the game.
But,
his heart's not in it
because he already knows
what the outcome will bring.

He's ordered to pass the ball
to the privileged players.
He stares
and watches them score.

And as applause rings out
the coaches and refs
stare back at him
because they know
he knows that their game is rigged.

# There Goes the neighborhood

I progress with modesty.
I desire with reservation.
I raise my voice with humility
and say sir, before I speak.
My stature in intimidating
so, I crouch when I talk to my boss.
Run all his demeaning errands
I strive to be accommodating at any cost.
I make my children play quietly
in the back yard.
Sometimes in the house
never out front
never at the park.
I drive my old car
keep my new one in the garage.
Don't want anyone thinking,
their new neighbor is living large.
Tip-toe on eggshells around my new environment
maybe they won't notice I've gained empowerment.
Careful not to make waves in my community.
Don't want to loose my new status
and end up back in poverty.

# What about Africa

I've never been to Africa
but I don't think it's for me-
Every time I read the paper
they show me death,
hunger, and retched poverty.
Can I visit a place
that reeks of waste
where children wallow in squalor
with open sores upon their face?
The old folks told me
that Africa was a land of splendor,
promise, and pride.
But all the images I see
are of hungry children,
dirty water, and flies.

In a magazine
I once read that-
most Africans
have never slept in a bed.
And that in a year
one million more Africans
would be dead.
Probably two,
is what they said.
And I think-
If I visited Africa
The whole time I'd be scared.

They always show
the animals in Africa

more happy than the people.
And I think-
Damn,
Who's showing me these pictures?
Because how can they
spend millions
for ratings when they're broadcasting
and not give a damn
about the people they pass by suffering?

On reality shows
Africans run barefoot
and half naked
and I think-
Does anyone wear high heels,
socks or boots?
Do they ever go to work
or to church in suits?

Are these the images
the media
wants me to see?
Or is it really
every Africans ugly reality?
Did my government forget
to share a little technology-
or serve up a little hospitality?
If countries in Africa
had half the oil of Arabia
I bet America would treat them
like Saudi royalty.

# Take it and leave

Agricultural rape,
Geographical plunder

You come to Africa-
you take our women
and leave your disease.

Take diamonds, take minerals, take animals
and leave souls with broken lives and shattered homes.

We see your airplanes take off from dirt airstrips.
Weighed down with all they can get.

You promised to bring back medicine-
said we'd all get better one day.

You feed me spoonfuls of hope
from bowls full of dreams.

Take samples of my soil
Take samples of my blood
Take rivers of my sweat.

Now you want to take pictures
with your arms around me.
Take your hands off me!

You got what you came for.
Just take it and leave-
Take it and leave!

# Bring the War Home

Bring the war home!

Let them see what they started-
Tell them what's not being reported.

Bring your guns, bloody rags, and unmended bones.
Wear the dog tags of your best friend
who aint comin' home.

Push his star spangled coffin
up and down main street again and again.

Let them see his mother crying.
Was her loss worth their gain?
Make the war hawks taste some of her pain.

Wear your fatigues that smell of gunpowder,
and your blood spattered boots.

Stand closer and closer
till the scent stains their suits.

A poor mans courage translates the risk.
While the business of war is cheered on
by cowards hiding behind a desk.

# Diversion

Who owns reality?
God
Satan
Or maybe just me.

Who controls destiny?
Dharma
Karma
Or maybe just me.

Who distributes grief and poverty?
Government
Corporations
Or maybe just me.

Who can limit individuality?
Church
State
Or maybe just me.

# Solitary Confinement

Trapped-
Trapped-
Caught between telling the truth and living a lie.

Space-
Space-
It's hard to find space.

Room to breathe
Room to live your own life without staying in the
confined
quarters of someone else's mind.

Trying to please someone
all the while hurting no one but ourselves.

# Prelude To An Addict's Prayer

Addict, ad-dikt, v. Someone with a physical or
psychological dependence. Hence
something you can't get enough of that's
not good for you. A very, very bad habit.
A craving. An out of control compulsion;
Desire that could ultimately lead to your
destruction, (or someone else's).

Also referred to as having a monkey on your back.

Examples:
| | |
|---|---|
| Heroin | Cocaine |
| Marijuana | Alcohol |
| Nicotine | Caffeine |
| Sugar | Sex |
| Gambling | Food |

Which addict are you? -

# An Addict's Prayer

Lord help me take today one hour at a time.

Keep me strong in the face of my enemies.

Help me keep my faith in the presence of adversity.

I will not regress and give in to this temptation

Set before me, as I do so struggle to progress

and set forth positive change for my life and the

life of my family. Give me wisdom.

# The Cigarette Smokers
## Hall Of Fame

Guidelines:

A.)   You must have smoked yourself to
      death.
B.)   Contracted throat cancer, lung
      cancer, etc. as a direct result of
      your cigarette smoking.

      1.Suffered like a 'dog' before you
      died, thereby making your story
      worst than most-which enabled your
      lawyers to draw more sympathy from
      jurors.

C.)   Family received a huge settlement
      from big tobacco, after proving
      your cigarette addiction is what
      ultimately killed you.

D.)   Your family must enjoy spending all
      that money your death made
      possible.

## Newlywed Couple With A Newborn
### Baby-Thinking out loud

Wife-  I wonder.....when he saw the stretch marks on my stomach and breast did he find me less attractive?

Husband-  I wonder if she's properly healed yet? It's been six weeks. Would she get mad if I wanted to try some breast milk?

Wife-  When the baby is hungry and cries during the night, does it distract him? Does it change his mind about touching me? Or is that just an excuse for him to stay on his side of the bed?

Husband-  I think I should shave before I turn in tonight. She likes my face nice and smooth. And if junior starts crying again tonight, he's going to have to wait. His mother and I have unfinished business from last night.

Wife-  When he gets home from work and my hair isn't done and I've got the same dress on, does he think less of me?

Husband-  Damn! Junior must have worried her to death again today. Better her than me! Maybe I should buy her a wig and a sexy new dress to help cheer her up. Where the hell is the remote?

Wife-  When dinner isn't ready, he gives me a funny look. When I ask him to feed the baby while I go in the kitchen and cook – Does he think I've gotten lazy?

Husband-  I'm starving to death! I should have surprised her and picked something up on my way home. I better write that down. Little Junior is a handful. I wonder how I can get out of changing this nasty ass diaper?

# Martha's Soul Kitchen

## This Weeks Menu:

Sunday
Babecue Chicken Wings
Sweet Squash
Cabbage w/ Fatback
Butter Beans &Corn
Chocolate Cake & Ice Cream

Monday
Fried Shrimp w/ Homemade Cocktail Sauce
Fried Fish w/ Hot Sauce
French Fries & Onion Rings
Hush Puppies
Sweet potato Pie

Tuesday
Fried Chicken w/ Hot Sauce
Mashed potatoes
Corn on the Cob
Barbecue Spare Ribs
Corn Bread
Sweet Potato Pie

Wednesday
Rib Eye Steak
Neck Bones w/ Fatback
Collard Greens w/ Fatback
Black Eye Peas w/ Fatback
White Rice & Carrots
Sweet Potato Pie

Thursday
Pork Chops w/ Gravy
Lamb Chops w/ Gravy
Ox Tails
Stuffing
Dirty Rice
Sweet Potato Pie

Friday
Hot Wings
Barbecue & Coleslaw
Barbecue Baked Beans w/ Fatback
Macaroni & Cheese
Corn Bread
Peach Cobbler & Ice Cream

Sunday
High Choloesterol
Clogged Arteries
High Blood Pressure
Stroke
Heart Attack
Hospitalization
Increased Insurance
Sweet Potato Pie

* Saturday night come early for our weekly raffle. Win a carton of Newport Cigarettes.

# I don't get around much anymore

Since I've changed
my young man's clothes
my mirror looks at me differently.
The man who owns this beard
is a stranger.
The man beneath this beard
is his brother
forever grown apart.
Reflect back –
glance over my shoulder,
this man I see
aint who I use to be.
I'm trapped in the body
of a man who is a father.
And this man is a husband.
And this man is a neighbor
who is nice and polite
and goes to church with his family.
I fill the shoes of a man
who is an employee of a
monotonous suburban machine.
Day in, day out
clock in, clock out.
Family van carpools
P.T.A, groceries.
Who's kids are these?
Damn, did I join a cult?
My old clothes don't fit.
Now I wear my father's

Stained shirt and leisure suit.
A husbands pleasant haircut too.
She even makes me cover up my tattoos.
Six pack turned into a keg.
Traded in for the family man stomach.
My single life is dead –
witness the birth of the family man.

# Everybody Wants Something

My wife wants me
to be a better husband.
My girlfriend wants me
to leave my wife.
My mama wants me
to leave my girlfriend.
My kids want me
to stay home more.
My brother wants me
to hang out with him more.
My brother's wife wants me
to be a better example for her husband.
And I just want them all to stop wanting.

# Empty

A kiss without passion
is like a touch without emotion
is like sex without climax
is like having a one night stand
with yourself.

# Mama

Mama
gave us sunshine
as soon as
we came
Through her womb.
Mama
lost future husbands
cause of her kids.
Mama
made sister's prom dress
with her own two hands.
Used her last dollar
to bond me out
of jail
that time I acted the fool.
I remember that day
Mama
fought the neighborhood bully
for me,
(and no she did not loose).
She always kept the rent man
at bay.
In seventeen years
we only went to bed hungry
one night.
Mama, wasn't just Mama –
Mama was Daddy too!

# At 18....

Daddy told me that –
a man ain't a man
until he stands for something
(So he took me to get registered to vote).

Mama told me that –
a man ain't a man
if he can't provide for his family.
(So she took me to fill out applications).

Grand daddy told me that –
a man ain't a man
until he kills something.
(So he took me hunting).

Grandma told me that –
a man ain't a man
if he doesn't have a talent or skill with his hands.
(So she got me enrolled in trade school).

My older brother told me that –
a man ain't a man
until he busts his cherry.
(So he took me to a whorehouse).

Which advice do you think I liked most?

# Absentee Father

Dear Absentee Father,

You were the coward who ran off but left me his name.
In your absence, God made me a man –
while you hid behind your mask of shame.

My soul never stirred when that name was mentioned.
Honestly, (and if you'd asked)
I never would have given you a chance at redemption.

So take this one thing with you to your grave;

This man who was raised by women –
grew strong, and has remained unforgiving.
This man is a loving father and parent to his children.

This man was a troubled man, but remained true.
A man who spoke with God –
the same God who will be waiting to judge you!

Never had the opportunity to call you dad.
And I never missed something I never had.

# Mama Sure Could Pray

When Mama opened her mouth at church
a lot of folks listened cause Mama
sure could prey. Mama asked God for

everything. She prayed for the church
members who were shut in. She asked for
the sick to be healed. And even for the
choir to sing like angels, which in itself

would be a miracle if you've ever heard
our choir sing. She prayed for everybody
who was in church that Sunday, including
the pastor – and for his sermon to be perfect.

When Mama got the Holy-Ghost, a lot of
"hallelujahs" came out while she was
talking. People in surrounding pews
joined hands and "hallelujahs" came out

of their mouths too. I wouldn't sit right
next to Mama in church, but I would be on
the same pew, because when the Holy-Ghost
got into Mama, she squeezed my hand too
hard.

And sometimes she prayed so fast, spit flew
from her mouth. When Mama finally said amen-
she looked really exhausted. She would some-
times be sweaty and hoarse.

And her feet hurt from standing so long. She
kind of looked like me after a few games of
basketball. And when everybody else opened
their eyes – everybody who actually shut their
eyes during prayer, their eyes were red.

As if they just woke up from a deep sleep.
Now, if you thought Mama could pray at church
You should have seen her at home. There were
15,20,30 minute prayers over breakfast, dinner,

when company came, when company left, when someone
was sick, or someone dies. She probably prayed them
straight into heaven. Even during thunderstorms
Mama turned off the t.v. and all the lights and
prayed while 'the Lord was doing his work'.

Sometimes Mama's prayers were answered,
sometimes they weren't. And the ones that
didn't get answered made Mama pray even harder.

If God handed out awards for people who
could pray, and who meant every word –
Mama would definitely win top honors,
because Mama sure could pray!

# When It Rains

I didn't think the sun was ever going to
come out. It rained all day and half the
night when we went to Rita's funeral. The
old folks say that when it rains during

someone's funeral, it means the angels are
crying, and that person is going to heaven.
But I don't know about that. 'Cause if that's
true, then my uncle Ron must have went straight

to hell. His funeral fell on the hottest day
of the year. Two people passed out while Rev.
Thomas was preaching. Maybe uncle Ron lived a
Secret life nobody knew about. Maybe the

weather man didn't know uncle Ron died and
forgot to make it rain – the real weather man.
And what about Deacon Scott who lived next
door to us? He use to make his dog attack

anybody who walked across his grass. The day
of his funeral, it was so cold, only ten people
showed up. Including the funeral directors
who didn't like having to help carry his

oversized casket. That day, sister booths' ankle
swelled up so badly, they had to rush her from
the cemetery straight to the emergency room.
Anyway, it didn't rain the day we attended his

funeral either. And he was a Deacon, who went to church twenty-six years. I think he smoked cigars too. I;m going to stop attending funerals. The guest of honor (for lack of a better word) can't see

or hear you. Casual people get all dressed up. And people who never gave a damn about you when you were alive, get to stand over you and stare down at you. The preacher always talks too long and most of

the time doesn't even know you.
(but the food is always good. Hummmmmmm)

If one day you should find yourself at my funeral, you have my written permission to wear whatever you like. Shorts, t-shirt, work boots, uniforms, hardhat. And tell Reverend or Pastor 'whats his name', to keep it short

and sweet. I'm sure you've got some place to be. And if it rains that day, you know where I'm going to be!

# Intervention

I'm the mother of two children
cut from the same cloth
lost to the same cause –
the streets.

I love them both the same
but I want them both to change –
their lives.

My son sells goods
my daughter sells services
they both have unusual clients.

My daughter's dirty deeds
do not go unnoticed by me.
In the dark, from my window, I see:
her.

Posing beneath the streetlights.
In and out of cars
her clothes are soiled and thin
her breath made foul from the stink of men.

My son's possessions and greed
do not go unnoticed by me.
In the dark, from my window, I see:
him.

Fill his pockets with a substance
of which I dare not speak.
Men and women of all ages
flock to his feet.

They have both made horrible decisions.

As children, this is not what their father
or me envisioned. But
since his death, they have both run a muck.
Since his death, they have both strayed so much
from God.

I love them both the same.
I beg them both to change –
their lives.

My daughter says –
"I'm grown,
I do what I want to.
I do what I have to,"

My son says –
"I'm a man,
a man's got to do
what a man's got to do."

So I asked God for help
and waited for him to
make things better.
And I waited and waited
Still he did not answer.

In the meantime:

My daughter's clients keep her up all night.
My son's clients keep him running all night.
On my knees, I stay up and worry all night.

I could not stand to watch, and do nothing.
I wanted to make sure redemption was
forthcoming.
I felt it was my Christian duty to intervene.

I thought God wanted me to stand between –
them and their worldly ways.

I got the police involved
and they both eventually went to prison.
That's right, I turned in my own children.
I felt it was the best decision.

Seeing them in court wasn't my finest moment.
I believed that upon their release,
they would thank me for it.

But –

Despite my best intentions,
they both denied my visits.

Something strange transformed them in prison.

Now, because of what I did
I have forever lost my kids.
They both disowned me as their mother.
Instead of becoming close to God,
they ended up further than ever.

Angry and blasphemous and
what's worse?
Their roles have been reversed.

Now my daughter sells goods,
and my son sells services.

# Farewell
## (for my brother Maurice)

Sleep thy deep sleep o' brother.
Thine days and nights hast merged into one continuous dream.
Only one voice can rouse thee from thy slumber now.

O' careless hands that plucked thee from us –
How I often despise thee, yet I am told by God that I must love
thee, in spite of suffering thou hast laid at my feet.

Thus I must see through my bitter contempt to grasp this
elusive love for thee, for I too am thy flesh and thy blood.
I too share thy shame.

The face of anger does not smile at his sister and grin at his
neighbor, yet frown at a stranger. But deals equally cold
stares to us all.

I designed these words and speak them gently. I dare not vex
others of our lineage. But my heart must speak its mind. Truth
bares no shame greater than denial.

My soul hast grieved three thousand days for thee dear brother.
Yet, I hold comfort in the knowledge that thine seeds hast grown
into beautiful flowers.

And from such seeds generations of flowers shall bloom. All
fertilized by thine blood, and hold thine ancestral name upon
their lips.

Thy last words linger near me, like the final entry in a lost journal. I recall them often at dawn, when sunlight warms my face. I see thee in the rays that thou so dearly loved.

Thou could hast been born a prince, or scholar, or clergyman or statesman, and I would have never known thee. But destiny knew thy name and my soul hast been made rich because of it.

It is with heavy heart that I bid thee farewell my brother. I know that thou hast gained God's favor, and he allows thee to shine down upon us, thy beloved and be grieved.

I rest, assured in the knowledge that somewhere, sometime, somehow, someday, thine eyes shall again meet mine.
And we shall talk and we shall laugh –

And we shall remember what was. And we shall again know better days.

# Insurrection

The end of this day Draws near And
I look to find shadows of hate
impeding my path.

They gaze at me through envious eyes.
They grin at me with crooked smiles.
They spew negativity at my feet.

When they try to break my spirit,
They shall hear me scream –

"I will not bow down to thee.
I will not live on my knees.
I will not beg you for your
tomorrows, I will create my own."

Spring forth hope from oppression,
shine bright light from depression.

Sing loud voices of children of hope –
of dreams – of passions unforeseen.
Remind me that I live and in living
I can breathe the breath of a new day.

I'll take giant steps into the unknown.
Open my ears to the untold.
No longer will I allow complicity
to torture my soul.

I will not waver.

I will not fold.

And though I may stumble,
I will not fall.

Run-
Cover your hate filled eyes.
That brilliant light you see holds sustenance
for all my people.

Though I bleed
My spirit will remain unbreakable.
My resolve steady and unshakable.
My voice resounding and unmistakable.

I say to all you who are able
come and stand with me.

## Truth In Fiction

The ordinary life
of an ordinary man
does not good fiction make.

But the unexpected experience
of extraordinary circumstance
can turn an ordinary man's life
into unbelievable truth.

Also available by julius Kane

"Ten Things Every Black Man Must Do
Before He Dies"

Visit;

www.maverick-publishing.com


Maverick publishing books are
distributed by Bookmasters
www.bookmasters.com